| DATE | | | |
|---|---|---|---|
|  |  |  |  |
|  |  |  |  |
|  |  |  |  |
|  |  |  |  |
|  |  |  |  |
|  |  |  |  |
|  |  |  |  |
|  |  |  |  |
|  |  |  |  |
|  |  |  |  |
|  |  |  |  |
|  |  |  |  |
|  |  |  |  |

# Making a Telephone

Published in the United States of America by Cherry Lake Publishing
Ann Arbor, Michigan
www.cherrylakepublishing.com

Reading Adviser: Marla Conn MS, Ed., Literacy specialist, Read-Ability, Inc.
Book Design: Jennifer Wahi
Illustrator: Jeff Bane

CIP data has been filed and is available at catalog.loc.gov

Printed in the United States of America
Corporate Graphics Inc.

**About the illustrator:** Jeff Bane and his two business partners own a studio along the American River in Folsom, California, home of the 1849 Gold Rush. When Jeff's not sketching or illustrating for clients, he's either swimming or kayaking in the river to relax.

## Science Notes

*Making a Telephone* explores how sound waves travel. In this experiment, the reader connects two plastic cups with a long string to make a simple "telephone." When someone speaks into a cup, the sound waves travel through the string, allowing the person on the other end to hear their voice.

The **telephone** is helpful. It lets you talk to people far away.

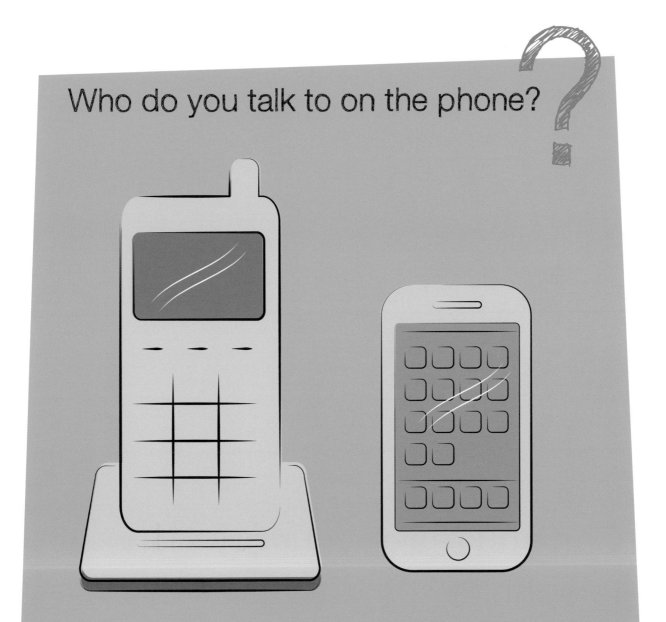

Can you make your own kind of telephone?

# Let's find out!

It will let you talk to someone in another room. It does not use **electricity**.

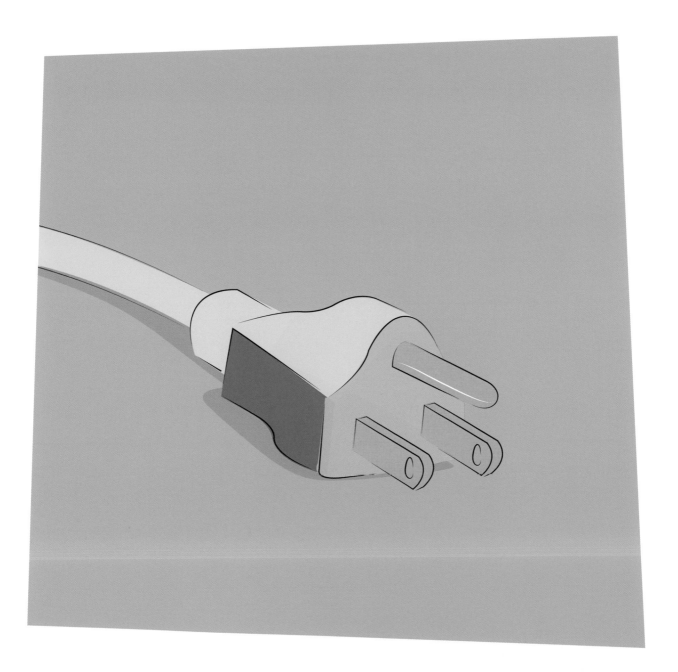

- Sharp pencil

- 2 plastic cups

- Long piece of string

- A friend

# You will need these things

Poke a hole in the bottom of one cup. Use the pencil. Stick the string through. Tie a **knot** at the end of the string.

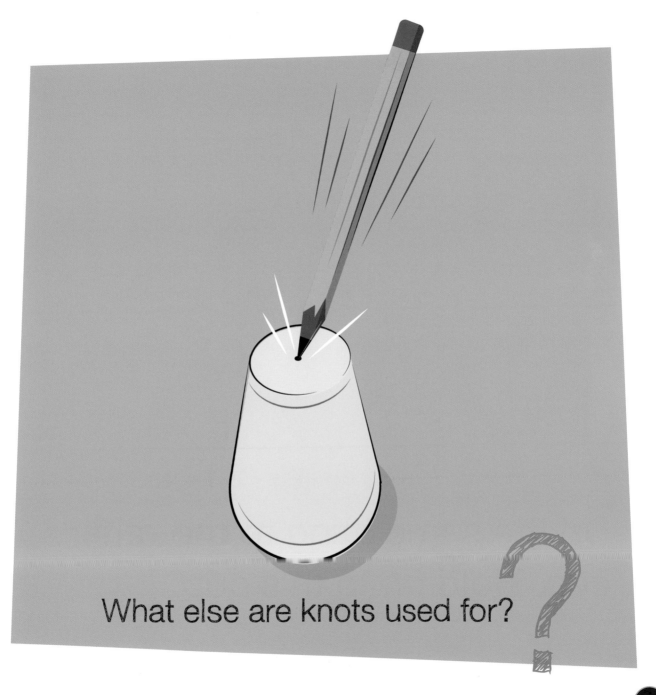

What else are knots used for?

Do the same thing to the other cup. Hold on to this cup.

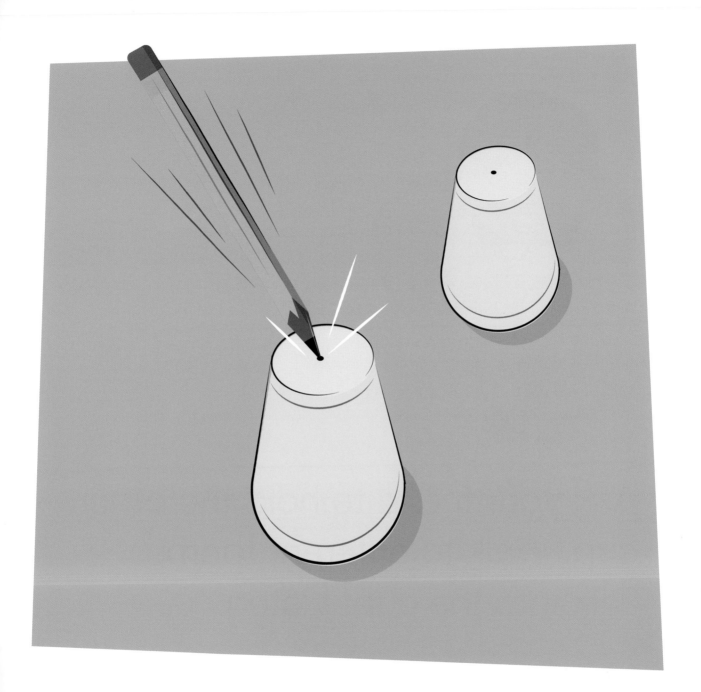

Ask your friend to hold the other cup. Walk to different rooms. Talk into the cup. Listen.

You can hear her talking through the cup.

# Why do you think this is?

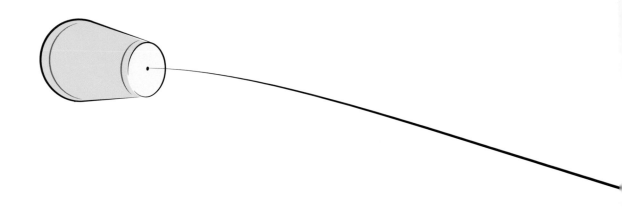

Try it with shorter string. Try it with longer string. Try different cups. What happens?

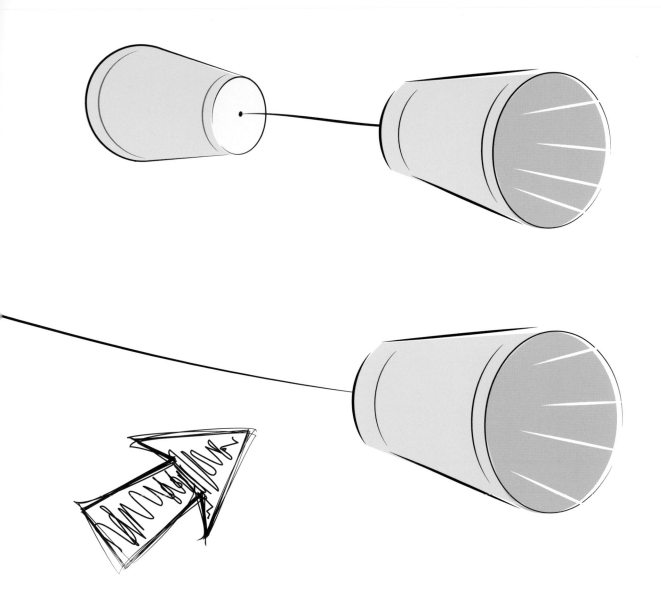

Try different strings!

Good job. You're done!
Science is fun!

What new questions do you have?

## glossary

**electricity** (i-lek-TRIS-i-tee) power that goes through wires to make machines work

**knot** (nawt) a piece of string tied to itself to connect two things

**telephone** (TEL-ah-fohn) a device that sends voices over long distances

## index